**Educational Heretics Press
exists to question
the dogmas of education in general,
and schooling in particular.**

The Next Learning System:

and why home-schoolers are trailblazers

by Roland Meighan

Educational Heretics Press

Published 1997 by Educational Heretics Press
113 Arundel Drive, Bramcote Hills, Nottingham NG9 3FQ

Copyright © 1997 Educational Heretics Press

**British Cataloguing in Publication Data.
A catalogue record for this book is available
from the British Library.**

Meighan, Roland
The Next Learning System:
and why home-schoolers are trailblazers

ISBN   1-900219-04-2

Design and production: Educational Heretics Press

Printcd by Mastaprint Ltd., Sandiacre, Nottinghamshire

Contents

This book is dedicated to the memory of Ivy Meighan

Other books by Roland Meighan

Roland Meighan began writing for public consumption in his mid-thirties because it was a requirement of his appointment as a university lecturer. He was, until recently, a long-standing editor of the influential journal **Educational Review** and author or co-author of over a hundred publications, including twelve books. Two of them, *Perspectives on Society* and *A Sociology of Educating,* have become best selling, classic texts.

Other well-known works of his are:
Flexischooling: Education for Tomorrow Starting Yesterday;
an edited work entitled *Learning From Home-based Education*;
Theory and Practice of Regressive Education;
a book of educational quotations entitled *The Freethinkers' Guide to the Educational Universe;*
a directory to alternative ideas entitled *The Freethinkers' Pocket Directory to the Educational Universe.*

His most recent work is *John Holt: Personalised Education and the Reconstruction of Schooling,* written as a tribute to Holt ten years after his death. He has written for a variety of audiences, in journals, for book publishers, for magazine readers and for newspapers.

Introduction

Schooling can seriously damage your education

This introduction gives me a chance to do several things. One is to 'pay my dues' and acknowledge the debt I owe to members of Education Otherwise and other home-educating families, for around twenty years of inspiration. This book declares some of the things I have learned from this association. Another task is to indicate the good news and the bad news about home-based education based on my own research and that of others.

In general, the good news is that it is possible to achieve an effective education in the UK, in the USA, and elsewhere too, and it does not matter which of the rival definitions of 'effective' education you adopt. The bad news is that you will probably have to do it yourself in the form of home-based education, for the evidence assembled in the pages that follow indicates clearly that school is now the second-best option. Choosing the 'best buy' of home-schooling can involve successes and strains, inspiration and grit, delights and despair, but, as one parent declared:

"A bad day at home is a whole lot better than a bad day at school."

(Computer bulletin board note from a home-schooling parent, quoted in *Home School Researcher*, Vol. 9. No. 2. p.1, 1993.)

Of course it must be **possible** to do it badly at home, especially if you try to ape the rigid and coercive models of knowledge and behaviour common in schools. As one learner observed:

"If we are going to continue doing this school junk at home, I might as well go and do it at school."

In earlier times, George Bernard Shaw had signalled his irritation at how schooling had diverted him from a better use of the time:

"My schooling not only failed to teach me what it professed to be teaching, but prevented me from being educated to an extent which infuriates me when I think of all I might have learned at home by myself."

Although it may be possible to do it badly at home, I have not personally witnessed any cases over twenty years that I would regard as deficient. They have been good, very good or outstanding. I guess that unsuccessful families are likely to 'cease trading' fairly quickly and opt back into a school.

On the other hand, I observe that it is **possible** to achieve effective education of each of the rival kinds in schools, but it is much rarer that you think, and mostly confined to a small number of democratic-tending schools, or particular classrooms with inspired teachers. So, there are oases in the desert, but mostly it is desert.

One aspect of this desert is that it is profoundly anti-democratic. It continues to be the case that, for the most part, we have totalitarian-style schools in our so-called democracy developing what John Taylor Gatto (1992) has described as the 'bad habits of schooling' in the learners:

"School is a twelve-year jail sentence where bad habits are the only curriculum truly learned. I teach school and win awards doing it. I should know. "

Outsiders spot this at once. *"Oh, it is totalitarian,"* my Polish colleague, Professor Eugenia Potulicka of Poznan University, told me when I asked her what her conclusions were about the UK schooling system. She went on to say:

"The 1988 Education Act is a very dangerous development for it has politicised schooling in the direction of fascist thinking. It is the worst development in Europe at the moment."

I have known people gasp at such a conclusion, yet the last European State to reinstate corporal punishment was Nazi Germany. In the UK, in 1997, we have strong calls to follow suit.

Effective education in its rival forms is more likely in early childhood stage in the state sector of England and Wales than in anything that follows, as my partner Janet keeps pointing out to me, but the 'poisonous pedagogy', as Alice Miller so graphically describes it, has gradually weakened its immune system since the 1988 Education Reform Act of England and Wales. Ann Sherman (1996) has shown in her study of five-year-olds' perception of schooling, *Rules, Routines and Regimentation*, that young children now absorb the messages of conformity and uniformity by the end of their first year in school.

I have said many times that my analysis should **not** be interpreted as an attack on teachers: teachers are all too frequently victims too. The system sometimes forces them into absurdities, such as this;

"One headteacher told John's parents to make his home life less interesting so he would not be so bored at school."

(in *Times Educational Supplement* 20/9/96 Features, p.3)

But, in the end we are left with the uncomfortable proposition that, in the UK, both state and private schools are, in the long run, more likely to do damage to a child's education than anything positive. Perhaps Mark Twain should have the last word:

"I never allowed schooling to interfere with my education."

We may be able to learn lots of negative lessons as the obsolete mass schooling system decays around us. But I prefer to learn some positive lessons from the home-schoolers. We shall not, however, be able to identify the result desired by people wanting the comfort of a One Right Way:

"Home-schoolers will not teach the schools what they so yearn to know, the one best way to do anything. What they will teach is that there is no one best way, and that it is a waste of time and energy to look for it; that children (like adults) learn in a great many different ways; that each child learns best in the ways that most interest, excite, and satisfy her or him; and that the business of the school should be to offer the widest possible range of choices, both in what to learn and ways to learn it."

(John Holt *Teach Your Own*, p.331)

Chapter one

Small beginnings

In 1977 a small group of 'educational heretics' met in a farmhouse near Swindon and set up a small co-operative that would provide mutual support to any attempts of its members at home-based education. It was to be known as **Education Otherwise**, the title being derived from the clause in the 1944 Education Act declaring that education was compulsory for children aged five upwards, either by attendance at school, **or otherwise**.

I was not able to attend the first meeting but joined in the next gathering in Worcestershire. Some group members, representing about ten families, had already started home-based education, others were considering doing so, yet others were concerned to give support to such an initiative.

The idea was not new, of course, as the following exchange indicates:

Interviewer: "You never went to school? Or you did for one day?"

Yehudi Menuhin: "Not even one day; one morning ... When I came back from the morning, my mother asked what I had learnt. I said, "I really didn't learn anything". I sat at the back of the class, and there was a little window high up on the wall, through which I could see branches. I hoped that a bird would alight. No bird alighted, but I kept hoping, and that's about all I could report. So my mother promptly said, "Well, we'll educate you at home."

(Yehudi Menuhin, July 1996, Radio Interview 'In the Psychiatrist's Chair'.)

What was new was extending the practice from aristocrats and the well-to-do, to 'ordinary' people. None of the early members of Education Otherwise had much in the way of material resources.

Similar developments were occurring elsewhere in the world, in countries such as USA, Canada, Australia, New Zealand and France. Later, linking up with these groups in other countries was to be an important source of encouragement, exchanges of experiences, articles, books and research. The group would also find that their 'heresy' was actually a criminal offence in at least one European country.

The numbers game

The second question people tend to ask is, "How many people are doing it?" The first question is, of course, "What about the social life of the children?" The only true answer to the question of numbers is the same in every country. Nobody knows. No country keeps accurate figures. Indeed, most do not keep any figures at all. The most prolific growth appears to be in the USA. Professor Philip Gammage, during a two-month long assignment teaching and researching in Virginia and Illinois in Spring 1996 was talking to the Superintendent of the Peoria School Board, Illinois. He asked Philip if he was aware of the remarkable growth of home-schooling. Philip was able to demonstrate a good working knowledge of the phenomenon - one of the benefits of being an Education Now Associate Director is that you are likely to be well-briefed in such matters! The Superintendent told Philip that 3% of the school-age population was now engaged in home-based education in his region. More and more arrangements for flexi-time were being developed to allow opting in and out of schools at will.

The figure of 3% is startling. When home-schooling, as it is known in USA, began to grow in the 1980s, it was confidently predicted by the experts that it would never grow to more than 1%, given that this was such an 'eccentric' idea and so demanding on the parents, who really had to love their children a lot to undertake such a task. Apparently more USA parents 'love their children enough' than the experts were inclined to believe!

On the current growth rate, it is now possible that as much as 10% of the school-age population in USA could be experiencing home-based education, either full-time or flexi-time, by the end of 1999. The confident predictions of the experts of a 1% maximum is already just another bad guess to be consigned to the garbage-bins of history.

In UK, the latest estimated figure from Education Otherwise is that 25,000 families, or 50,000 or more children, are engaged in home-based education and this is approaching 1% of the school-age population. In UK too, the numbers are growing at over 100 families a month and could reach 3% by the turn of the century.

A quiet revolution

We can see that in the UK and USA, and in various other countries an unusual, quiet revolution has been taking place in the form of 'home-schooling'. At the same time as the fierce debates about mainstream education have been taking place concerning the National Curriculum, Testing, 'Back to the Basics', Opting Out or Opting In, Local Management of Schools, etc., some families have just quietly been getting on with a 'Do It Yourself' approach to education.

This phenomenon is more accurately described as **home-based education** because the majority of families use the home as a springboard into a range of community-based activities and investigations, rather than try to copy the 'day prison' model operated by the majority of schools.

People find this quite hard to grasp, and this is shown in the asking of the inevitable first question about whether such children become socially competent. After only a little reflection, it is clear that learning activities out and about in the community give children more social contacts, and more varied encounters, as well as reducing the peer-dependency feature of adolescent experience, sometimes known as the 'tyranny of the adolescent peer group'. Thus the reality is quite the opposite of the belief: it is the school-based who get the restricted social life rather than the home-based.

People often react to news about home-schoolers by trying to generate generalisations and stereotypes about families educating the home-based way, their social class, their incomes, their life styles and their attitudes. The only ones that the evidence supports are:

- that they display considerable diversity in motive, methods and aims,
- that they are remarkably successful in achieving their chosen aims.

Schools often take up the posture that if home-based education is to be tolerable, the families should learn how to do it from the 'professionals'.   The evidence is different and demonstrates that schools often have more to learn from the flexibility of many families, than vice versa.

One reason for this is that when schools were set up, we lived in an information-poor environment.   Today we live in an information-rich environment.   This is a major factor in contributing to the success of home-based education.   Then, schools were designed to produce rather rigid, conformist people on a production-line model.   Today we need flexible, adaptable people and the production-line approach is not noted for this.

Chapter two

Home-based education effectiveness research

The year 1977 is when Education Otherwise began, but it also marks the start of research into home-based education in England and Wales. This research was to become a steady accumulation of case studies. Some surveys were undertaken by asking members of Education Otherwise to fill in questionnaires, and research students used a variety of samples for their studies.

In the USA research also began about the same time, although it was 1985 before the journal *The Home-School Researcher* was established. The research in the USA has, for the most part, taken the form of systematic survey analysis. The researches in the two countries complement each other in style, but are similar in findings, because the general conclusions are almost identical.

Since 1977 the central question researchers have asked has changed. At first, the concern was whether home-schooled children would be able to match the performance of children at school. The issue was whether parents were putting their children at a disadvantage by their home-based education programmes. If they were, it was implied, they might have to be over-ruled. Indeed, in the one country that has never waited for the evidence, and where home-schooling is a criminal offence, it has been reported that children have been taken to school in handcuffs.

As the evidence came in, it became clear that home-schooled children performed much better than their school-based counterparts, being on average two years ahead on any aspect tested, and up to ten years ahead in above average cases.

There was concern in one study by Jack A. Sande (*Home School Researcher* Vol 11, No. 3, 1995, p. 7) that showed that home-schooled children *were not as far ahead* in mathematics tests as they were in other tests:

> *"Most home-schoolers scored significantly higher than both their public school counterparts and national norms, but math scores showed the least advantage."*

The implication of this research was that children should be discouraged from attending school, because they would be at an inevitable disadvantage - the reverse of what had been feared! Instead of such conclusions being drawn, however, the question began to change. It became: "Why were home-schooled children so successful?" Chapter three of this book provides some of the answers.

This book as a whole marks the adoption of a third question. What can we learn from the trail-blazing activities of home-schoolers to develop a better learning system suited to the needs of life in the 21st century?   The final two chapters take up this concern.

The evidence from the systematic studies

1. The issue of social skills

One edition of *Home School Researcher*, Volume 8, number 3, contains two research reports on the issue of social skills. The study by Larry Shyers found that home-schooled students received significantly lower problem-behaviour scores than schooled children. His next finding was that home-schooled children are socially well adjusted but schooled children are not so well adjusted.

Shyers concludes that we are asking the wrong question when we ask about the social development of home-schooled children. The real question is that of why the social adjustment of schooled children is of such poor quality.

In the second study, Thomas Smedley used different test instruments but came to the same conclusion: that home-educated children are more mature and better socialised than those attending school.

Some possible reasons emerge from this study:

- The classroom, after the early childhood stage, offers mostly one-way communication often of a stilted kind and few meaningful interchanges are in evidence. In home-based education the opposite is the case.

- Schools are products of the factory age with batches of uniform products running on the conveyor belt in lockstep motion towards the standardised diploma. It therefore socialises into this kind of mentality. Home-based education, in contrast, works to more personalised educational outcomes.

- An unnatural aspect of school is age segregation. Learning to get along with peers alone does not prepare students for varied interactions with older and younger people in life. Home-based education avoids this trap for in the home-school learning programmes, people of various ages are encountered out and about in the real society.

- The emphasis of home-based education on self-discipline and self-directed learning and the personal confidence this produces, creates young people who can adapt to new situations and new people.

The question of how home-schooled children fare as adults has been the subject of a study in the UK by Julie Webb (1990) and in one in the USA by J. Gary Knowles. The study of 53 adults who experienced home-based education was conducted by Knowles of the University of Michigan (1993). He found that more than three-quarters of the sample had felt that being educated at home had actually helped them interact with people from different levels of society.

The adults appeared to be 'satisfied customers'. When asked if they would want to be educated at home if they had their lives over again, 96% replied 'Yes'. The factors that were commonly highlighted by the adults concerned were:

- the self-directed curriculum,

- the individualised pace of working,

- the flexibility of the home-study programme.

Not one of the sample was unemployed or on welfare assistance, and two thirds were married - the norm for the age group.

Knowles concludes that the idea of there being social disadvantages to home-based education was not supported by the evidence. Indeed, the evidence suggested the reverse.

2. The issue of intellectual and academic development

The academic excellence of home-schooled children has been repeatedly demonstrated in the research in the USA and also confirmed by the case study material in England and Wales. In summary, the earlier findings were that they consistently score at or above the 50th percentile on standardised achievement tests, with more than half scoring at the 70th and 80th percentile. (Alaska Department of Education 1985, 1986; Hewitt Research Foundation 1985, 1986.) Later studies from the USA put home-schooled children at least two years in front of their schooled counterparts in intellectual achievement and sometimes as much as ten years ahead (Ray 1991).

Few people, I find, seem to dwell on the academic issue and they rather tend to assume that the efficiency of home-based education is likely to lead to superior academic results. The experience of parents in having to shore up the inefficient learning systems of schools by supporting endless homework activities, means they do not need much persuasion about this fact. Even if their personal memories of school have faded, their children will often have made them aware that school learning environments are limited, and often rather hostile. It is the other aspects, such as social education, that people question.

3. The competence of parents as educators

Home-based education groups in USA are, from time to time, in dispute with some officials who are trying to make it a condition that a parent has to be a certificated teacher. A research study by Joan Havens in 1994 supports the home-schoolers because it shows that the certification of parents had virtually no impact on learning performance.

The factors that she found to be more decisive in explaining why children learning at home do so well on academic tests are:

- low teacher-student ratio

- close supportive contact between parent and child

- the individualised methodology

- the freedom of the student to interact independently and creatively with the curriculum.

The study by Havens included another attempt to check out the academic success of the home-schooling families and it comes to the same conclusion as the others; i.e. that the children scored significantly higher on the Stanford Achievement Tests than schooled children in the locality:

> "This study focused on the academic aspects of home-schooling. It demonstrated that, for the sample selected, achievement was higher for home schooled children than for traditionally educated students."

Havens found that it was the high interest and involvement of the parents in the educational process that was significant rather than qualifications.

4. Competence in science

Hornick (1993) studied a group of seven families with teenage children in Massachusetts to find out how science was learned in home schools. He found that the parents in the sample did not teach science to their teenagers: the teenagers taught themselves. The result was 'inquiry science of the very highest quality'. The students performed as real scientists in exploring phenomena, making hypotheses, designing and carrying out tests and analysing and evaluating results. The memorising of texts and the getting through worksheets was not found to be in evidence in the study programmes of the learners, but textbooks were used as a source of ideas and reference.

The families saw science as a 'hands on' activity. Science shows on television were used extensively and trips to science museums, farms, nature centres and national parks 'were a staple of the science curricula'. The parents, whose own backgrounds in science were rather slight, learnt with their children rather than giving any instruction. They saw themselves sometimes as learning coaches and sometimes as fellow inquirers.

Parents operated with a sense of the 'teachable moments' when their teenagers' interest and curiosity had been aroused. Every family agreed that locating suitable resources was the key to their science learning and this was the justification for the extensive use of TV and field trips.

Hornick's assessment of the scientific knowledge and understanding gained was that it was of the highest standards but that the families were largely unaware of this and rather took the quality of their learning for granted:

> *"When I asked 13 year-old Louis what science he knew, he neglected to mention that he is an expert at identifying medicinal herbs and preparing oils and tinctures; for him this was his small business not science."*

5. Competence with computers

The study by Marchant (1993) of the use of computers by home-schoolers was unusual in its research approach. It had three parts to it:

- The first consisted of a summary of data obtained from a directory of those home-schooling families interacting through an education bulletin board.

- The second was a content analysis of the notes posted on the bulletin board.

- In the final part, other researchers joined Marchant in posting questions to the home-schoolers on-line and the responses were analysed.

He found that 185 families from 37 states were exchanging ideas and information on a regular basis without ever physically meeting. The characteristics of this group were analysed without any assumption being made that they were typical of the general population of home-schoolers.

Marchant found that this group was knowledgeable and sophisticated. The parents were a fairly well-educated group who felt that their own formal education had contributed little to their success as home-educating parents. They were well equipped in terms of modern computer technology and know-how, and even though they tended to downplay the importance of this, the impact on the competence of the children was hard to ignore.

Marchant notes that negative experiences with schools had left many of the parents in his sample discouraged and angry. They were unresponsive to suggestions that schools could be improved.

> *"As the author expressed his hopes for bettering public education and continued to request ways to improve public education from the home-schooling parents, the conversation ended."*

6. A study of factors that might effect home-schooling

The study by Terry Russell, reported in *Home School Researcher* (Volume 10, number 1, 1994) checked out some of the factors that might contribute to the widely recorded academic success of the home-educated. Russell asked nine questions, and surveyed the existing research on these, before studying 877 home-school parents in the Washington area. This is a lengthy paper using some complex statistical techniques and it needs to be consulted in original form to get into the detail. In summary, his findings are:

(a) Does family income influence academic achievement?
It does not have any measurable effect and family income is not a predictor of academic success as measured by the SAT (Stanford Achievement Test).

(b) Does the parent's level of education have any effect?
The effect of parent's education, measured by years completed, was small, although this was the single best predictor.

(c) Does the student's previous grade level have an effect?
There was no evidence in the analysis to suggest that students of previous lower or higher grades respond better or worse to home-based education.

(d) Is the number of years a student has been home-schooled an influence?
This was not shown to be a factor in academic performance in the SAT. (The average length of time for the sample was 2.7 years, with a standard deviation of 1.5 years.)

(e) Does the previous type of education have an effect?
There were no measurable effects except some small effects relating to structured learning (see below). Of the sample, 28.5% had been previously in private schools, 39% in state schools, 30.8% always home-schooled and 1.5 % 'other'.

(f) Does whether the parent has had training in home-schooling make a difference?
This particular study related to a local training class and showed no measurable effects except a marginal effect relating to structure (see question eight).

(g) Does the amount of religious content incorporated in the curriculum have an effect on academic achievement?
No effect was measurable. (40% had a strong religious identity, 42% weak, and the rest none.)

(h) Does the amount of structure used have an effect?
The SAT assumes a structured approach to learning, so it was to be expected that there would be some interesting issues. The amount of structure used in the home-based curriculum did have a small positive effect on the scores recorded in the SAT. Parents who want their children to perform well in such tests, are, on the evidence of this study, advised to be aware of this.

(i) Does the number of hours per week spent in home-schooling have an effect on student academic achievement?
No measurable effects were found. The average time spent on timetabled study was 15 hours, with a range of 0 to 45 hours.

Russell concludes that, in line with previous studies, none of the factors examined in this study asserted a powerful influence on the success of home-based education. This study indicates yet again, that there is no reason to doubt that the home-schooled students in the sample are receiving a very good education.

7. Research from Canada

In 1993 the Francombe Place Research Associates undertook a survey of home study in Canada, state by state. The author D. S. Smith obtained responses from the Deputy Ministers of Education and the 30 home-schooling associations in Canada. He found that home-schooling was firmly entrenched and officially recognised as an acceptable educational option. Official records showed about 10,000 registered families but estimates from the records of the associations suggested more like 30,000 since many families do not register.

Smith was interested to see if the next generation would home-school. The response was positive and typical responses were that 'when I get married and have children of my own I will definitely home-school'. One reason was that the order of priorities was seen as different:

> *"Our order of priorities is often the reverse of the ordinary world. We **begin** with happiness." (p.71)*

The diversity of parents involved was apparent:

> *"They are, by any classification, a diverse lot: housewives, teachers, doctors, back-to-the-landers, lawyers, francophones, anglophones, fundamentalists, ministers, farmers, and just plain parents, of all faiths and creeds. All of whom are united in one common belief: they are concerned about their children and their children's education. Concerned enough to do something about it themselves." (p.15)*

As studies in other countries have found, the motives and methods of these home-educating families are also diverse but the success rates are increasingly undisputed:

> *We know home-schooling works for those who are prepared to invest the effort. We know it has inherent values. We know it is not for everyone."*
> *(p.57)*

8. A UK study of learning methods

Alan Thomas became interested in home-based education through *Education Now* and we first met because of a mutual concern for the logistics of individualised learning. One family had volunteered themselves for study and Thomas took up the offer. The study was so illuminating that he extended its scope. He interviewed 23 families in the Greater London area and carried out observations of 10 of them. The research is ongoing and also involves a sample of families in Australia (Thomas 1994).

Parents were asked to share in the joint venture of exploring how their children learned. Observations were mainly undertaken in the kitchen, where so much home-based education in the form of conversations takes place and it was recorded with pen and paper. The qualitative data was subjected to content analysis to identify emergent themes.

Families starting out on home-based education who at first adopted formal methods of learning found themselves drawn more and more into less formal learning. Families who started out with informal learning at the outset found themselves drawn into even more informal learning.

The methods that both groups grew into had much more in common with the methods of learning in younger children. The sequencing of learning material, the bedrock of learning in school, was seen increasingly as unnecessary and unhelpful.

Learning to read was a central concern, but parents showed less anxiety when their children showed no inclination to learn at the usual age:

> *"Curiously, these children who learned to read relatively late still went on very quickly to read material suitable for their age. Most of the children were voracious readers."*

Thomas stresses that his work is in the early stages and should not be regarded as the last word on the matter. Nevertheless, he is already aware that his research challenges one of the fundamental assumptions of schooling:

> *"This study challenges the almost universally held view that children of school age need to be*

formally taught if they are to learn. In school this may be the case but at home they can learn just by living."

The changing scene

In the UK there have been several changes since a handful of families first began to co-operate to form the organisation Education Otherwise in 1976. These include:

- changes in motivation,

- changes in acceptance by Local Education Authorities,

- rapid and substantial growth in numbers,

- changes in the questions posed by the home-based education phenomenon.

As we saw earlier, the basic question of 'Will the families cope?' has given way to 'Why do they usually cope so easily and so well?' Home-based education effectiveness research demonstrates that children are usually superior to their school-attending peers in social skills, social maturity, emotional stability, academic achievement, personal confidence, communication skills and other aspects.

The lessons of this research, as to how the schooling system could be regenerated, are only just beginning to be appreciated. It questions all the fundamental assumptions under-pinning schooling. It then points to ways of regenerating and reconstructing education systems in general, and schools in particular, in the direction of the flexibility that is a requirement in the post-modernist scene. It gives us clues as to how we can de-school schools by developing a network of learning sites to replace the obsolete mass, compulsory, and custodial school.

Home-based education effectiveness: the evidence from case studies

The research undertaken by myself and several of my research students since 1977 has included:

(a) collecting information from questionnaires sent to members of Education Otherwise,

(b) interviewing families ,

(c) telephone interviews,

(d) making notes at meetings of home-based educators,

(e) collecting newspaper, magazine, radio and TV. reports,

(f) research students collecting data for their theses,

(g) preparing detailed case studies for lawyers defending families.

As a result, a considerable bank of information has been built up and scrutinised. The patterns that appear in the data have been analysed and reported elsewhere. (see Meighan (1984), Webb (1990), Lowden (1993).) The case study material generates a variety of information about home-based education which complements the findings of the systematic studies found in the USA literature in all the key features.

Famous people studies

One approach is to assemble evidence about cases in the past and make reference to the achievements of people educated this way. Some are well known people, some living, some dead, such as Yehudi Menuhin, Patrick Moore, Agatha Christie, Margaret Mead, Thomas Edison, George Bernard Shaw, Noel Coward, C.S.Lewis, Pearl Buck, Bertrand Russell, John Stuart Mill, Winston Churchill. There are many more.

Contemporary successes

Reference can be made to current academic successes gained by home-based students; e.g. in England, Sarah Guthrie's daughter admitted to York University, the Everdells' son admitted to Cambridge, and the Lawrences' daughter admitted to Oxford aged 13, Aliah Blackmore gaining prizes at a University in London, the Clawley family with one studying for an Open University degree and the other at the University of Warwick.

The World-wide Education Service results

Reference can be made to the World-wide Education Service (WES) of the Parents National Education Union founded by Charlotte Mason because they have been educating children at home and abroad for over a hundred years by means of a correspondence course for the parents using similar principles of distance teaching to those of the Open University.

Court case verdicts

Reference can be made to the crucial court case Harrison v. Stevenson in 1981, that led to the judge deciding that the Harrison family's home-based education was a success:

> *"They are mature, confident and at ease in all sorts of company. They are lively minded, have a good general knowledge and are intellectually athletic ... In their case their education - in its own field- has proved and is proving, a marked success."*

'In its own field' meant that the Harrison family had elected for autonomous education based on practical and self-sufficiency skills rather than an academic approach.

In the USA, John Holt's book *Teach Your Own* carried a wealth of material about court cases in various States and the publication *Growing Without Schooling,* published by Holt Associates, continues to do so.

Teachers who home-educate

My own interest in home-based education was not detached and aloof. My son was approaching five years, the usual school-start age in UK. As a teacher myself, with 'insider knowledge' of the limitations of schooling, I began, alongside my wife Shirley, who taught infants in a primary school, to look at alternatives.

We found that private education was, with a few honourable exceptions, even more oppressive than state schooling at that time, and that its morality was highly suspect both because of its divisive elitism and its fascist-tendency ideology. (We found in our investigations, that Hitler admired British private schools, which he saw as producing the kind of mentality needed in the officers of the Third Reich. The two books by Chris Shute, (1993 and 1994), explore these tendencies at some length.)

Home-based education looked by far the most interesting possibility. At this point we got wind of the first meeting of Education Otherwise.

We were not the only teachers to come to this conclusion and another source of reference is that of the presence in the ranks of the home-based educators of so many members of the teaching profession - at least 25% of the cases at any given time, and currently about 33% in the UK - who have decided that home-based education provides the best option for their own children.

Home-based education effectiveness: the evidence from a personal review

Researching home-based education has been a remarkable experience that has helped me personally to review most of my assumptions as a practising teacher about educational matters. Some of my early hunches became supported by the evidence of my own eyes as I visited families who were 'home-schooling':

- Diversity without exclusiveness is likely to be healthy
  - because individuals differ and families differ
  - because circumstances are different
  - because successful education can take many forms.

- Therefore **always** suspect regimental One Right Way 'answers' - such as the 'answer' of a British National Curriculum, or 'salvation by phonics', or 'salvation by testing'.

- Wounds can heal and children can recover from bad learning experiences especially in the supportive environment of a concerned family. I have witnessed this too many times now to think it is an unusual event.

- It is actually hard for a school as currently organised to match an alert, organised and energetic family. Only a few schools even get near it, as I was able to observe as I went from studying home-educating families to supervising students in school and back again for over ten years.

- Flexible learning, (and as a result the production of flexible people), is currently more likely to be found in home-based education.

- Learner-managed learning (autonomous education) is at present more frequently found in home-based education: school tends to focus down on 'how to be taught' whereas homes tend to teach 'how to learn'. Schools, therefore, tend to teach you to be stuck with the gaps in your knowledge, homes how to fill them.

- Confidence-building is currently more likely to be found in homes.

- Non-sexist education can be achieved more easily at home than under the present models of schooling.

- The habit of peer-dependency and the 'tyranny of the peer group' produced by school operating the current officially approved model can be reversed by home-based education.

- The rotation and alternation of a variety of types of curriculum is commonplace at home, but currently much rarer at school.

- Co-operative and democratic forms of education are more likely to be found in home-based settings because of the dominance of the authoritarian management model in schools, as portrayed in *Beyond Authoritarian School Management* by Lynn Davies (1994).

- So-called 'school phobia' is actually more likely to be a sign of mental health, whereas school dependency is a largely unrecognised mental health problem.

- Homes are more likely than schools to achieve, *'The child in pursuit of knowledge and not knowledge in pursuit of the child'*. (George Bernard Shaw).

- A few families have one child in school and another out, with options to change in either direction based on experience and needs. They are pioneering a more flexible form of education. One positive way forward for the schooling system may be to take up the idea derived from home-based educators of flexi-time and ultimately flexischooling.

Home-based education effectiveness: A school pupil's view

This letter from a child in school, quoted in an Education Otherwise Newsletter, points to some of the effective features of a home-based education observed from her point of view:

Dear Education Otherwise,
My best friend is Susan and she doesn't go to school; she is taught at home by her parents and is more interesting than someone that does go to school because she knows a lot more.

I sometimes feel a bit jealous of her, because she is more educated than some of my other friends and myself. At school there are quite a few bullies, but Susan doesn't have to worry about things like that. Sometimes I wish I was educated at home as well as Susan and her brother, Paul, as they can spend more time with their parents and pets.

At school, you hardly use a computer, but Susan and Paul nearly always use a computer and are shown how to use one properly. They are always learning about new things - at school I always learn about the same things over and over again!

Some teachers are hard to get on with and you don't get any encouragement from them, but your parents always give you encouragement.

Carol Ann, aged 12, from Bolton

Home-based education effectiveness: An official view

A letter from Boston University Undergraduates Admissions Director proclaims:

"Boston University welcomes applications from home-schooled students. We believe students educated primarily at home possess the passion for knowledge, the independence, and self-reliance that enable them to excel in our intellectually challenging programs of study."
(in Smith, D. 1993, p.4)

Message in a textbook

In 1995 a textbook, *Home Schooling: Parents as Educators* by Maralee Maybury, J. Gary Knowles, Brian Ray, and Stacey Marlow, Thousand Oaks, California: Corwin Press Inc., was published. In UK, it was available via Sage Publications, London.

This book provided some answers to intriguing questions about the rapid and sustained growth of home-based education in the USA, then the choice of over one million families. Why was this happening? What are the characteristics of the home-schoolers? What are their motives and their methods? The book drew heavily on the accumulation of *The Home School Researcher*, then in its 11th year.

The most striking finding replicates that of the accumulated case study research in UK. It is that of diversity. Families differ widely in their motives, their methods, their aims, and their learning plans. The main thing they have in common is that they are remarkably successful in achieving whatever they set out to achieve.

The diversity is also reflected in the variety of support groups in USA. The organisation Holt Associates, *"serves primarily liberal, secular, and humanistic home education families"* and other associations exist to support the families with *"conservative and Christian parent educators" (p.25)*. The division of families appears to be about 50/50 in USA, with half the families professing a strong religious motive and others much weaker or none. This categorisation can be deceptive, however, for some of these 'religious' families state that their motive is primarily educational rather than religious.

The profile of home-educating families in USA shows a tendency towards middle-income, young, and well educated, which is defined as having some years of completed study in higher education institutions. But plenty of *"parents with less education and fewer financial resources are also teaching their children at home. In many ways, home-schooling is an educational choice that appeals to a wide spectrum of people." (p. 34)*

One other thing families have in common is a marked degree of scepticism and lack of confidence in social and public institutions including schools, banks and other financial institutions, major companies, the press and the media, governments, the unions or the courts. (p. 40)

I recommend this book, even if, in the end, it is rather non-radical. The over-detached, clinical form of analysis serves to squeeze out most of the excitement and enthusiasm I personally have experienced in researching and working with families in UK. The joy of families who succeed in restoring both the sparkle into the eyes of their children and the zest for learning, by their home-educating, is somehow missing.

The key question of how families can be so remarkably successful is not seriously addressed in the book. It is the growth of an information-rich environment in particular, as well as other factors like the recent communications revolution, which makes so many homes more effective, efficient, and learner-friendly learning settings. As a consequence, the need for schools to abandon the current totally obsolete compulsory factory model and become flexible, democratic and invitational, does not emerge. In consequence, there is talk about families dealing with schools **as they are,** rather than pointing to how schools have to be reconstructed in order to respond to the trail-blazing activity of the families.

Chapter three

Why is home-schooling such a success?

(a) Natural learning and 'dovetailing'

Families educating at home often engage in highly sophisticated activity without necessarily being able to articulate what they are doing. Most parents find, as John Holt proposed in *Learning All the Time,* that young children are 'natural' learners. They are like explorers or research scientists busily gathering information and making meaning out of the world. Most of this learning is not the result of teaching, but rather a constant and universal learning activity 'as natural as breathing'. Parents achieve the remarkable feats of helping their children to walk and talk by responding to this process. This is, perhaps, the most successful example of educational practice world-wide. In the first five years of life, astonishing learning takes place as a non-verbal infant learns its native language, to walk and to achieve competence within its home and local environment. All this achieved, with varying degrees of success, by so-called amateurs - the parent or parents and other care-givers such as grandparents.

The highly sophisticated activity of parents is described as 'dovetailing' in to the child's behaviour. Parents appear to have no pre-determined plan of language teaching, they simply respond to the cues provided and give support to the next stage of learning - as the child decides to encounter it.

(b) Direct access to an information-rich society

When schools were set up we lived in an information-poor society. Therefore getting children together in one place to give them access made some kind of sense. Now that we live in an information-rich society, it makes little or no sense as Richard North (1987) observes:

> *"We no longer have to force-feed education to children: they live in a world in which they are surrounded by educative resources. There are around 500 hours each of the schools' television and radio every year in this country. There are several million books in public libraries. There are museums in every town. There is a constant flow of cheap or free information from a dozen media. There are home computers which are easily connected to phones and thus other computers...There are thousands of work-places... There are... the old, the disabled, the very young all in need of children in their lives, all in need of the kind of help caring and careful youngsters can give, and all of them rich sources of information about the world, and freely available to any child who isn't locked away in school."*

Although the information-rich society is a world-wide phenomenon, some societies in the majority world are still relatively information-poor. The implications of home-based education are less clear in these circumstances. Yet the arrival of high-tech clockwork radios and ultimately computers, is likely to be a significant breakthrough here.

(c) The adaptation to a wide variety of learning styles

Given the fact that we are able to locate over thirty differences in individual learning styles, any uniform approach to the curriculum or to learning is intellectual death to some, and often most, of the learners, and is therefore suspect.

Human beings, adults and children alike, differ from each other quite dramatically in learning styles. To date, thirty two such differences have been catalogued. An example would be the difference between those who learn better with some background noise and those who learn better in quiet conditions. Individuals also differ in the kind of light conditions, temperature conditions, bodily positions, food intake and type of companions needed for efficient learning. Bio-chronology is another factor, for some are early-day learners and some late-day or evening/night learners.

Therefore, the situation in which one teacher faces thirty children in one room and is required to deliver the same material within a given period of time, say forty five minutes, to all of them, means that drastic harm to the quality of learning of many of the class and the resultant loss of a great deal of potential learning, is inevitable.   In contrast, in the home-based education I have witnessed, the families rather take it for granted that learning styles differ, and vary the learning situations accordingly.

(d) Efficient use of time

When I have interviewed children who have come out of school into home-based education, I have asked them to compare the two experiences.   Usually the first response is the comment on efficiency of learning.   They say that they have frequently learnt more by coffee-time at home than in a whole day at school, so that the rest of the day is 'additional learning'.   This helps explain why children who are 'behind' at school soon catch up at home, and also why they can end up two to ten years ahead of their schooled counterparts.

(e) A non-hostile learning environment

It is not just efficiency that the children note.   They have told me about the relaxed atmosphere at home which encourages them to be increasingly confident in taking over the management of their own learning.   When they started school at five years of age, we know they were asking about thirty knowledge or enquiry questions an hour, but that this soon drops and eventually gets to around zero.   In the non-hostile home-based education, they tell me, their interest in learning and curiosity and questioning begins to build up again.

By contrast, the main effects of the 1988 Education Reform Act in UK have been to create much more hostile learning situations for the majority of children.   It is hardly necessary to argue the point - almost every newspaper, radio station and television channel carries reports each week of school exclusions, unhappy children, unhappy parents, and teachers queuing up to take early retirement.   John Holt even forecast that this might happen in 1975:

"A majority want the schools to be even more rigid, threatening, and punitive than they are, and they will probably become so." (p. 58)

I recently ran a day course for student teachers on 'alternative ideas in education and the next learning system'. The gathering was very subdued from the start. Then the story began to unfold. Not one of the students wanted to go into schools and develop a career in teaching because of the way the task had been presented to them in the previous months. *"I just do not want to go into schools and do the things to children I have been ordered to do"* one student volunteered. The others agreed. The task had been presented in terms of what C. Wright Mills described as the 'cultural mechanics' task - to bolt on to children bits of selected information and then test whether they had stuck on.

This echoes the verdict on the previous UK National Curriculum of the late 1800s which ran for about thirty years. Its designer was the Senior Chief Inspector, Edmond Holmes. When he retired he wrote a book condemning the whole of his previous thirty years' work. Holmes observed that under a National Curriculum approach, learning and teaching became debased:

"In nine schools out of ten, on nine days out of ten, in nine lessons out of ten, the teacher is engaged in laying thin films of information on the surface of the child's mind and then after a brief interval he is skimming these off in order to satisfy himself that they have been duly laid."

The 1988 UK National Curriculum looks very much like the 1870s version both in subjects and in the 'tell them and test them' methodology.

(f) Learner-managed learning: plan, do, review

The success of the Ipsilanti High Scope programme has been widely published. Children in schools using this approach are encouraged in the basic skills of deep learning; that is, they learn to plan, do and review. What has been overlooked is that home-based education usually operates to the same principles and is therefore equally successful in producing competent and confident learners. By adding the efficiency factor mentioned above, however, the home-based pupils are likely to pull ahead.

John Holt, in *Teach Your Own,* lists some of the principles he has observed and advocates in the learning approach of parent who are home-schoolers:

> *"For a long, long time, people who were good at sharing what they knew have realised certain things: (1) to help people learn something, you must first understand what they already know; (2) showing people how to do something is better than telling them and letting them do it is best of all; (3) you mustn't tell or show too much at once, since people digest new ideas slowly and must feel secure with new skills or knowledge before they are ready for more; (4) you must give people as much time as they want and need to absorb what you have shown or told them; (5) instead of testing their understanding with questions you must let them show how much or how little they understand by the questions they ask you; (6) you must not get impatient or angry when people do not understand; (7) scaring people only blocks learning , and so on." (p.52)*

(g) The use of the catalogue curriculum approach

At least six different types of curriculum can be identified. The logistics of each of these types has been outlined elsewhere (Meighan 1988, 1993). All the various types of curriculum can be on offer at the same time in the **Catalogue Curriculum.** Others may have used this description before, but I have not come across it. Don Glines has something similar in his 'window- shopping' approach to the curriculum, and the 'shopper's guide' for students in his *Creating Educational Futures* (McNaughton and Gunn, Michigan 1995).

The learners, whether in schools full-time, or in flexi-time schooling plans, or full-time home-based education, are offered a catalogue of learning opportunities. The catalogue may be printed out for scrutiny or just made available, and it includes a variety of approaches:

• set courses, of the National Curriculum kind,

- ideas for making your own courses,

- instructions as to how to set up a learning co-operative,

- self-instructional packages,

- ways of getting access to other available learning resources and opportunities.

This approach to curriculum has been adopted by most families for their children between the ages of nought and five and by many families in their home-based educational alternative to schools after the age of five.

A catalogue curriculum approach is adopted by all the families I have researched myself. Without being able to articulate the theory, they utilise a variety of elements in their programmes. Often the morning programme may be imposed and pre-planned, sometimes to satisfy the wishes of the Local Education Officers, sometimes for external examination purposes, and sometimes for reasons of the family's own. The afternoon programme may then be of another kind; consultative, negotiated, or democratic in co-operation with another family. These families have already field-tested the catalogue curriculum.

An essential part of the approach of the families working in these flexible ways is the regular monitoring and evaluation of their curriculum. In some cases I have seen this taking place regularly and deliberately at morning coffee breaks supplemented by reviews at meal times. In other cases the planning and review has taken place in a regular Sunday evening meeting to decide the learning programme in outline for the following week.

(h) Matching the logic of Multiple Intelligence Theory

The case for the catalogue curriculum can be linked to the most recent research into learning. Howard Gardner in *The Unschooled Mind* identifies at least seven types of intelligence. Charles Handy in *The Age of Unreason* suggests that there are more than this. We have known for many years that there are more than thirty learning styles in humans. For these and other reasons, traditional education with its model of schooling devised in the age of the coach and horses, is obsolete. Most of the public debate about education can be likened to trying to make the stagecoach go faster by fixing roller-skates to the hooves of the horses.

The flexibility a full-blown catalogue curriculum approach implies is now widely recognised as the way forward in order:

- to equip individuals so that they can cope with a rapidly changing world, creatively and imaginatively, rather than with fear, obstructionism and fatalism,

- to match the wide variety of individual learning styles, learning biographies, forms of intelligence and learner aspirations,

- to match the needs of the modern economy for flexible, capable and adaptable people,

- to match the needs of a modern, living democracy for people who can operate as participating citizens exercising responsible, informed choice, and acting with all the necessary possible positive tolerance needed to make an open and diverse society work.

(i) Adults as learning agents, learning coaches, and learning site managers

When adults quiz the parents about home-based education they often ask how one or two parents can replace the team of experts of a school staff. Apart from pointing out that we live in an information-rich society now, so what the teachers know is available anyway, parents go on to describe themselves as 'fixers' or 'learning site managers' who help arrange the learning programme. They may also operate as learning coaches, or as fellow learners researching alongside their children, rather than as instructors. John Holt gives a useful summary of the qualities required:

> *"We can sum up very quickly what people need to teach their own children. First of all, they have to **like** them, enjoy their company, their physical presence, their energy, foolishness, and passion. They have to enjoy all their talk and questions, and enjoy equally trying to answer those questions. They have to think of their children as*

*friends, indeed very close friends, have to feel
happier when they are near and miss them when
they are away. They have to trust them as people,
respect their fragile dignity, treat them with
courtesy, take them seriously. They have to feel in
their own hearts some of their children's wonder,
curiosity, and excitement about the world. And
they have to have enough confidence in
themselves, scepticism about experts, and
willingness to be different from most people, to
take on themselves the responsibility for their
children's learning." (p.57)*

(j) Plenty of first-hand experience

The research studies quoted earlier indicate that first-hand experience is important in the approach of home-schoolers to learning. Thus, in the studies of the use of computers and of science explorations, those involved in home-based education just take it for granted that large amounts of first-hand experiences are essential to achieve effective learning.   This may set the parents up in another role as transport managers:

*"The parents' role in home-schooling is not to be the
fount of all knowledge ... Our role is to be enthusiastic
and experienced learners, role models for our children,
providing support and advice - and transportation to the
library."*

(British Columbia Home-schooler, in D. S. Smith *Parent-
generated Home Study in Canada,* p.70, 1993)

(k) The application of the various forms of discipline

People sometimes think that discipline is the simple problem of adults making children behave to instructions. This is only one kind of discipline - the authoritarian. Three kinds of behavioural discipline, (as well as several kinds of knowledge discipline) can be identified. They are:

1.   **Authoritarian** - where order is based on rules imposed by adults. Power resides in an individual or group of leaders.

2.   **Autonomous** - where order is based on self-discipline and self-imposed rational rules. Power resides with the individual.

3.   **Democratic** - where order is based on rules agreed after rational discussion; i.e. based on evidence, human rights values and the logic of consequences. Power is shared amongst the people in the situation.

There has been a centuries-old debate about which of these three is the best system of discipline. It is now a sterile debate.

The complexities of modern life are such that **all three types of discipline** have a place to play in the scheme of things. In some situations we need to be able to cope with **authoritarian discipline** and behaviour either by taking a lead or taking instructions. At other times we need to co-operate with others and behave with the **democratic discipline** of evolving and agreeing rules and then implementing and policing them collectively. Sometimes we need to be self-directing, take decisions for ourselves and act with **autonomous discipline**.

The same variety is found in knowledge disciplines. Sometimes we need to have memorised information using subject disciplines and at others to know the discipline of how to research to find knowledge. It follows that an effective education requires experience of all these approaches and an awareness when each one in turn is appropriate.

The experience of families educating at home has demonstrated how this can be achieved. The learners sometimes direct their own studies. At other times they work in co-operation with others and on other occasions decide to submit to instruction. The parents occasionally act as instructors, and at other times as facilitators, sometimes as co-learners, and often as sources of encouragement.

As before, families may not be able to articulate the sophisticated nature of their activity. But only a few schools, mostly the best of the nursery and infant schools, can match either the discipline variety or the curriculum variety of a home-educating family.

(l) Social Skills obtained from the real world

In the previous chapter we noted that a considerable amount of the research into home-schooling has looked at the social aspects. The findings are consistent in showing that the social skills, social maturity and emotional development of home-schooled children are superior.

This raises the question of how the myth that mass compulsory authoritarian schooling is a social maturing experience can be sustained any longer.   The reality is that we have actually constructed and sustained at massive public expense a machine for keeping children artificially immature.   This is achieved by consigning them to the influence of the equally immature minds and behaviours of members of their peer group, by imposition, for 15,000 hours, in an authoritarian organisation.   Chris Shute (1993) has graphically described this as *Compulsory Schooling Disease: How Children Absorb Fascist Values.*

The result is that the bully mentality is produced.   The problem with most discussions about bullying is that the root causes are overlooked.   School, based on the current model of the compulsory day-detention centre, is itself a bully institution.   Next it employs a bully curriculum - the compulsory National Curriculum.   This is 'delivered' by the increasingly favoured bully pedagogy of teacher-dominated formal teaching, which in turn is reinforced by the bully compulsory testing system.   All this requires a bully inspectorate.   The unwritten, but powerful message of this package, is that *the adults get their way by bullying.*   This bullying is by psychological and emotional coercion for the most part, but the call for physical bullying in the form of physical punishment is never far away.

There are at least three types of outcome.   The 'successful' pupils grow up to be officially sanctioned bullies in dominant authority positions as assertive politicians, doctors, teachers, civil servants, journalists and the like.

A majority of the 'less successful' learn to accept the mentality of the bullied - the submissive and dependent mind-set of people who need someone to tell them what to think and do.   John Holt describes this as the school's general course in Practical Slavery.

A third outcome is the production of a group of free-lance bullies who become troublesome and end up in trouble of varying degree of seriousness.

Amongst the reasons families give for starting home-schooling is that of getting away from bullying. Sometimes this is bullying by teachers, sometimes by children, sometimes it is by both, and sometimes by the dulling effect of a whole oppressive school regime. What families may not articulate is the escape from the long term effects of exposure to the bully mentality, briefly outlined above, but examined at greater length in Chris Shute's book and in Alice Miller's *For Your Own Good.*

(l) We now know more about how the brain actually works

One of the groups to have taken these ideas seriously is Accelerated Learning Systems Ltd. In *Accelerated Learning for the 21st Century,* Colin Rose and Malcolm J. Nicholl provide a survey of the evidence in a chapter entitled, 'The Awesome Brain'. They then apply some of the research findings to the design of their learning materials:

"The objective of Accelerated Learning is to:
a. Actively involve the emotional brain - thereby making things more memorable.
b. Sychronise left and right brain activity.
c. Mobilise all eight intelligences so that learning is accessible.
d. Introduce moments of relaxation to allow consolidation to take place. "

I find it is somewhat uncanny that the home-schoolers I have investigated, although they may have no knowledge of modern brain research, have already worked out some of the consequences in their practice. Often, they are already using most of the principles of accelerated learning in their learning programmes.

Colin Rose and Malcolm J. Mitchell of Accelerated Learning Systems stress the importance of confidence-building and self-esteem in their book. One of the most notable features of home-schooling is precisely such an outcome. When I have appeared on television or have made a radio broadcast in the company of home-schoolers, the presenters and staff have always remarked on the maturity, poise and self-confidence of the children.

But we do not have to rely on anecdotal evidence here, because the systematic studies in the USA demonstrate the same outcome. In a study of 259 families in Delaware, Vicki D. Tillman (1995) replicated the findings of an earlier study by Taylor in 1986 that:

> "... the self-concept of home-schooled children was significantly higher ..."

Tillman notes that the home-schoolers in her study were not isolated but active, contributing members of society, even in their childhood. She concludes:

> "If socialisation can be measured by good self-esteem, home-schoolers in the Delaware Valley are doing well."

Conclusion

Perhaps the reason for the title of this book is now becoming clearer. If we look at the reasons why home-schooling is so successful, they are linked with the latest research findings on multiple intelligences, the insights of modern brain research, the consequences of the move into an information-rich society, and the direct access made possible by the new technology of the communications revolution. The home-schoolers are indeed blazing a trail to the next learning system, in demonstrating how a more flexible approach to learning works in a variety of dimensions.

Chapter four

The heresy of home-schooling

The 'educational heretics' who met in the farmhouse near Swindon on 1977 did not know how things would develop. They saw their task as something like 'bringing happiness to a few children' rather than blazing a trail to the next learning system. Events have been on their side, however, since it has become obvious to more and more people, that mass compulsory schooling is obsolete. People who begin to find that they can learn more in hours on their home computers than they can in days in school, are bound to start to question what all the public money spent on mass schooling is achieving.

When I gave lectures on the theme of the obsolescence of compulsory mass schooling in the 1980s the idea was strongly resisted. Today, the response is more likely to be reluctant but widespread agreement. This is then followed by disbelief that we can devise a better system. This is no surprise to John Taylor Gatto, the author of *Dumbing Us Down: The Hidden Curriculum of Compulsory Schooling,* who sees that the imagination and creativity of people who have gone through the current system is likely to have been crippled:

> *"It is the great triumph of compulsory government monopoly mass schooling that among even the best of my fellow teachers, and among even the best of my students' parents, only a small number can imagine a different way to do things."*

1. Mass schooling - the end game

In an article written by Don Glines of the Educational Futures Project, USA, he asked whether mass schooling could survive for long into the 21st century. He thought not. A new synthesis was inevitable because of new information and new technologies.

(a) We now know of thirty different learning styles in humans

As we saw in the previous chapter, there are many learning styles. These learning differences fall into three broad categories, cognitive, affective and physiological. Some learners have a style which is typically deductive in contrast to those whose style is usually inductive. Others learn best from material which is predominantly visual as against others who respond best to auditory experiences. There are contrasts between impulsive learners and reflective learners. Some learn better with background noise, others in conditions of quiet. The work of Colin Rose and Malcolm J. Nicholl has taken this issue seriously in the design of kits that help learners to identify their most effective style of learning.

(b) We now know of at least seven types of intelligence

Howard Gardner in his book *The Unschooled Mind* (1991) reports his work on multiple intelligences. Seven types of intelligence (analytical, pattern, musical, physical, practical, intra-personal, and inter-personal) are identifiable. Only the first is given serious attention in UK schools. Charles Handy in *The Age of Unreason* (1990) declares:

> *"All the seven intelligences, and there may be more, will be needed even more in the portfolio world towards which we are inching our way. It is crazy, therefore, to use only the first of the intelligences as the criterion for further investment in any individual by society."*

We now know that so-called 'ordinary' people are capable of feats of intellectual or creative activity in rich, challenging, non-threatening, co-operative learning environments and the narrow competitive tests currently in use to achieve 'the raising of standards', just prevent this from happening.

(c) It is now clear that in a complex modern society, all three behaviour patterns and forms of discipline - authoritarian, autonomous and democratic - are needed

Effectively educated people need the flexibility to turn to each of the three major forms of behaviour and discipline described earlier. In different situations different forms of discipline are appropriate. People schooled in only one form of behaviour are handicapped in the modern world. As I indicated in *Flexischooling* (1988), rigid forms of schooling produce rigid people, flexible forms are needed to produce flexible people. Rigid university experiences build further rigidity of mind and behaviour on this foundation. As John Abbott points out in *Education 2000 News*, June 1996:

> "... we continue to get graduates who think narrowly, are teacher-dependent, and have too little ability to tackle challenges or embrace change. The situation makes us wonder whether the traditional classroom is right for the task - the need may be less for "reform" than for fundamental redesign of the system."

(d) Adaptability has priority in a rapidly changing society

There is now widespread recognition that with rapidly changing technologies, economies and life-styles, there is a chronic need for adaptability and flexibility in learning and in behaviour. A system based on uniformity is, therefore, counter-productive.

(e) The recognition of the need for life-long learning

The idea that essential learning is best concentrated between the ages of five and sixteen, and for some up to twenty-one, has increasingly given way to a recognition of the necessity for life-long learning.

(f) The arrival of the information-rich society

When mass schooling was established, people lived in an information-poor environment. Assembling large numbers of children together in one place called a school, with teachers who had been exposed to the scarce information, made a kind of sense. Since then, radio, television, the explosion of specialist magazines, computers, videos and the like, have all provided the means of making most of the products of the knowledge explosion readily available to anyone who wants it. This is just one of the reasons why home-based education is so successful and why its practitioners outperform school with relative ease.

(g) Democratic schooling has become an international concern

After the demise of State Communism in the former USSR and Eastern Europe, new governments look to schools in USA, UK and elsewhere hoping to find democratic models of schooling in operation. They find, to their surprise, the familiar model of authoritarian schools, which are not just non-democratic, but anti-democratic. After all, a key feature of democracy is the principle that those who are affected by a decision have the right to take part in the decision-making. This is expressed in slogans such as *'No taxation without representation!'* If we apply this to schools, we get:

> *'No learning and therefore no curriculum without the learners having a say in the decision-making'.*

In the authoritarian approach to schooling, however, there is a chronic fear of trusting students and sharing power with them, and a fear of opting for the discipline of democracy. Carl Rogers in *Freedom to Learn in the 80s* noted that democracy and its values are actually **scorned and despised**:

> *"Students do not participate in choosing the goals, the curriculum, or the manner of working. These things are chosen for the students. Students have no part in the choice of teaching personnel, nor any voice in educational policy. Likewise the teachers often have no choice in choosing their administrative officers ... All this is in striking contrast to all the teaching about the virtues of democracy, the importance of the 'free world,' and the like. The political practices of the school stand in the most striking contrast to what is taught. While being taught that freedom and responsibility are the glorious features of our democracy, students are experiencing powerlessness, and as having almost no opportunity to exercise choice or carry responsibility."*

It seems obvious that communist and fascist regimes will organise schools on an authoritarian or a totalitarian model. But it does not seem clear why a supposedly democratic regime organises on the same model, rather than adopting a democratic model. My Polish colleague, Professor Eugenia Potulicka, a specialist in Comparative Education, spent some time in England studying the

1988 Education Reform Act. I asked her what she would tell her university colleagues in Poznan, the Polish Government and the Solidarity Education Committee about the schooling system in England. Earlier, I gave her reply. It is worth repeating:

"Oh, I shall tell them it is totalitarian. The 1988 Education Act is a very dangerous development for it has politicised schooling in the direction of fascist thinking. It is the worst development in Europe at the moment."

(h) We now know much more about how the brain actually works

The new technologies allow us to watch a living brain at work. As a result, most of the assumptions of behavioural and cognitive psychology are in question. As John Abbott explains in *Education 2000 News*, June 1996:

"Studies in neurology challenge the common metaphor that the brain is like a linear computer, waiting to be programmed ... the metaphors of choice are increasingly biological - that is, the brain as a flexible, self-adjusting organism that grows and reshapes itself in response to challenge, with elements that wither away through lack of use."

In summary

The new synthesis derived from the effects of these ideas, means a new learning system with more flexible patterns. The new situation demands **alternatives for everybody all the time.** People trying to persist with the domination of the inflexible authoritarian approach of mass schooling are consigning our children to the obsolescence of the rigid mind-set.

2. The academic curriculum - the end game

I mentioned earlier that nowadays, my thesis that compulsory mass schooling is obsolete, meets less and less opposition. There is more shock, if not actual horror, however, at the proposal that the **academic curriculum is also obsolete.** Many parents are busy stoking up the expectations of their children that pursuing grammar school type curriculum will get them jobs. They are misreading the sign. The sign is beginning to say, in Monopoly board game style, 'Go straight to obsolescence, Do not pass Go, Do not collect a job.'

(a) An army of clerks

The point of academic schooling, whatever the rhetoric proclaims, has been to produce an army of clerks. Those who left at 16 with their examination certificates would go to work as bank clerks - as I did myself for a few years. Alternatively, they would become insurance clerks, or building society clerks, or something similar.

Those who left after the sixth form with 'A' levels, would go on to slightly better paid jobs in accountancy, or local government, or the like. Those who went on further and obtained a degree became top paid clerks in the civil service, government, law and elsewhere.

These former safe paths into jobs are now treacherous. Every time a bank, building society or insurance company announces its annual profits, it also announces the dismissal of more clerks. Thus, banking has now less than half the workforce of clerks than it did a few years ago. Moreover, the 'new' clerks in direct banking by telephone are **not** recruited for their examination prowess, but for their personal confidence and verbal, telephone skills. Indeed, examination success is often seen as a **negative** indicator that the prized independence and conversational skills may have withered or been sacrificed in the 'tell them and test them' machinery of school and university.

Another development is voice recognition technology which is now fully operational. Law firms are amongst the leading customers for voice recognition technology which enables them to dispense with the services of ... clerks. Case preparation software means that law firms can manage with half the number of lawyers, if they so choose. What applies to law firms applies to many others.

If further indication is needed about the decline of the academic pathway, the recent survey (1996) by the St Mungo Association of the homeless, and mostly workless, adults in its hostels, shows that 50% have academic qualifications, and 10% have a degree. In a recent lecture I gave the illustration that undergraduates struggling to get through university by working part-time at McDonalds, sometimes find that graduate unemployment forces them to go on to work full-time at McDonalds on graduation - not quite what they had been led to expect. A voice from the audience said, *"Tesco's - in my case it was Tesco's."*

(b) The end of work

For those who find enjoyment and satisfaction in the academic curriculum, it should, of course, be available as part of the catalogue curriculum. It is now becoming a lie, however, to claim that it will guarantee jobs. Indeed, the US economist and advisor to the US government, Jeremy Rifkin, warns us in his book, *The End Of Work*, that we may move into a situation where only a minority of the generation currently in the early stages of its school journey, can have **any** kind of job at any given time.

John Holt saw some of this coming. He noted in the growing obsolescence in 1971, even before computers really got to work on wholesale clerk-job demolition:

> *"The case for traditional education seems to me to be much weaker than it has been, and is getting ever weaker, and the case for an education which will give a child primarily not knowledge and certainty but resourcefulness, flexibility, curiosity, skill in learning, readiness to unlearn - the case grows ever stronger."*

> *(The Underachieving School, p.31)*

(c) An obsolete methodology

The clerk mentality is produced most effectively by the whole class teaching approach. The method has a low efficiency rate as regards learning. As noted earlier, the short-term recall of material taught this way is usually in the region of 5 to 10%. For long-term recall the figure is halved. By increasing the technical skill of the instructor, it is possible to get the figure for short-term recall up to 20%, and for long-term recall, 10%.

I refused to believe this as a young teacher and threw myself into getting better results than this. The pre-testing and post-testing showed that the research was correct and I could not refute it in my own practice.

The illusion that this approach is more efficient than this is sustained by two factors. One is that the most effective way to learn material is to teach it. The teacher remembers as much as 90% of the lesson! Because the teacher remembers it so well, he or she can easily slip into the illusion that the students do too. They do not.

The second factor is that the method is **shored-up by homework**. The recent studies from the Pacific Rim countries extolling the virtues of whole class teaching also show that two hours homework before school and at least two more hours afterwards are common.

(d) Lethal side-effects

Whole class teaching and the 'tell them and test them' approach in general, is not only inefficient, it has *lethal side effects*. It produces the gridlock mentality - dependent learners addicted to the right answers provided by authority. Those of us who have had to teach undergraduates and graduates from the Pacific Rim countries have often encountered the 'gridlocked' mind-set, the clerk mentality, at its fiercest. The rigid mind-set of many British undergraduates, however, can be a close rival.

Russian educators have also expressed concern at this mentality. *"Soviet children normally demonstrate better results in mathematics and science..."* than their counterparts in UK and elsewhere, Froumin tells us in *Creating and Managing the Democratic School* (edited by Judith Chapman, Isak Froumin and David Aspin 1995, London: Falmer Press). Nevertheless, he and his fellow writers want to abandon the authoritarian school, imposed curriculum, whole class teaching pedagogy (shored up by heavy doses of homework) and the testing that is responsible for these results, because they deliver **the wrong kind of person**. They produce the servile, authority-dependent outlook, and people good at selected mental tricks, rather than the democratic, life-long learning and flexible mentality.

Neither the Russian nor the Australian scholars writing in this book want to follow the British reforms of the last few years, for they see them as totally misguided and counter-productive. They appeared to agree with my Polish colleague's verdict.

Alice Miller sees this mind-set as the product of the *'the poisonous pedagogy'* and tries to make us face up to its lethal side effects.

Chris Shute in his book, *Alice Miller: The Unkind Society, Parenting and Schooling,* reminds us that Alice Miller found that among all the leading figures of the Third Reich, she was not able to find a single one who did not have the schooling and the strict and rigid upbringing that produced the gridlocked mentality. Carl Rogers added a further warning:

> *"People who cannot think, are ripe for dictatorships"*

3. The catalogue curriculum

"The idea of a National Curriculum has little educational merit and a poor track record." When I wrote this in *The Freethinkers' Pocket Directory to the Educational Universe,* there were plenty of squeals of protest.   But I actually thought I was being a bit restrained, because I take the view that the National Curriculum is an *anti*-educational concept and part of the regressive educational agenda.   This kind of judgement puts the onus on a critic to provide some alternatives.   I have done this elsewhere; e.g. in *Flexi-schooling* (Education Now Books 1988).

The lines of analysis are clear enough.   An adult-imposed curriculum, whether national or not, is part of the authoritarian approach to education.   The democratic and the autonomous approaches have different concepts to offer and different forms of curriculum.   Although these can be, and are, given technical sounding names, we need an analogy that connects with people.

In this endeavour, I have proposed the idea of the **Catalogue Curriculum.**   The learners are offered a   catalogue of learning opportunities, which can be published if required.

Because the catalogue includes pre-planned, negotiated and individual options, it serves the requirements of both the democratic and autonomous approaches whilst also allowing authoritarian offers to be included.   It thus serves the flexi-schooling synthesis, (Meighan 1988), which is an attempt to incorporate the advantages of all three types of discipline and learning approaches.

There are several operating examples of the catalogue curriculum approach in existence, although none of them, to my knowledge, is quite as broad-ranging as that I have in mind. Thus, the *City as Schools* initiative in USA presents its students with a catalogue of hundreds of opportunities for work experience/learning at work placements and any associated college-based course options, from which they devise their personal study programme in consultation with a tutor.

A second example is that of the Duke of Edinburgh's Award Scheme which has a catalogue of ideas for the skills part of the award, where a wide range of interests that can be pursued are described. A long-standing example is that of the Scout and Guide Movement and their catalogue of badges that can be attempted. This particular example shows how an authoritarian approach can be dominant - all the badge options are pre-planned recipes for learning.

Of course, the catalogue approach is common in Further and Higher Education. Further Education Colleges all produce a prospectus and the Open University, the UK's leading teaching university, is the best example of a catalogue approach to devising your own degree programme.

Nursery schools use a catalogue approach but it is not necessarily written down, except for the benefit of teachers in their planning sessions and for parents, since the learners are usually at a stage of early-reading.

In a previous life as a L.E.A. Evening Institute Organiser, I found that the preparation of the catalogue, the assembling of a team of part-time course leaders, and the booking of the various venues for the groups to meet, took up most of the summer months. It was a shoestring operation, of course; one full-time organiser, an assistant organiser half-time, and a full-time secretary, to service more than 10,000 local adult learners.

The case for the catalogue curriculum to replace all versions of imposed set curriculum, including any version of a National Curriculum, or even an International Curriculum, if we ever matured enough to get beyond our ethnocentrism, is based on the most recent research into learning. As we saw, Howard Gardner in *The Unschooled Mind* identifies at least seven types of intelligence. He has since added another. We noted that there are more than thirty learning styles in humans. For these and other reasons, traditional education, with its model of schooling devised in a different age, is obsolete.

On the other hand, the flexibility that a full-blown catalogue curriculum approach facilitates, is now more functional for the individuals in their changing society.

4. 'The domination of print literacy' - the end game.

The arrival of voice recognition technology is likely to move us gently and inevitably into a new oracy age.   This technology breaks the domination of print literacy.   Of course, books and other reading material will still be useful and will not disappear, but their domination is gone.   Machines can read and write for us occasionally, or most of the time, or all of the time as we choose and according to the situation.   The arrival of voice recognition technology is already transforming the world for many dyslexics and others with print literacy problems.

To some extent the decline of the use of print for information and entertainment has already started and has been replaced by TV and radio, for more and more adults and children.   As John Holt noted:

> *"From the fuss we make about reading, one might think that this was a country of readers, that reading was nearly everyone's favourite or near-favourite pastime.   Who are we kidding?   A publisher told me not long ago that outside of three hundred or so college bookstores, there are less than one hundred true bookstores in all the United States." (Freedom and Beyond p. 229)*

The development of advanced telephone technology, including the arrival of mobile telephones, has already had the effect of moving activities away from the print literacy skills into more use of oral skills.   An obvious example is the growth of telephone banking. Then, the arrival of book-reading technology for blind people, is equally usable by the sighted with reading difficulties.   There are more developments to come, such as the use of virtual reality and the next generation of wallet-size computers.

Thus, the move from an era of the domination of print-based literacy into a new era where oral literacy will be more central, is already under way, even if its significance has not yet been widely recognised.

Conclusion: Home-schoolers are ahead

The research evidence examined earlier placed home-schoolers ahead in conventional tests - on average, two years ahead of their schooled counterparts. If we look at the characteristics of the changing world, however, it would seem that they are being prepared for it effectively - by coincidence as much as design.

The flexibility of learning methods most families adopt and the varied curriculum that emerges, turn out to match the logistics of such things as the catalogue curriculum, multiple intelligences, and the variations in personal learning styles, leading to the flexibility of behaviour and mind that the modern world demands.

Chapter five

The next learning system

There are various groups around the world that have been at work on ideas for a new learning system suitable for the next century. They include the Educational Futures Project USA, Education 2000 UK, Education Now UK, TRANET International based in USA, and AERO USA. For example, the TRANET annual report for 1996 says:

"Thinkers in every walk of life are recognising that our current form of governance threatens ecological, political, social, and economic failure ... Management guru Peter Drucker says in his Post Capitalist Society "there is a need to restore community." He sees a new community-centred society ... in which schools are replaced by an open life-long learning system which any person can enter, at any level, any time ...

The 'Learning Community' theme is echoed by holistic educators who now recognise that 'child-centred education', much as it is needed for the flexibility inherent in the age ahead, is inconsistent with 'schooling'. 'Teaching' or 'schooling' implies that society, or someone is acting on, indoctrinating some amorphous blobs. 'Learning', on the other hand, implies a self-actualised process of creating skills, taking in knowledge, and satisfying one's natural curiosity ... Learning, like politics must be reinvented.

The vision of a 'World Without Schools' is being developed by organisations such as the Educational Futures Project. Schools fade into the background as the community as a whole becomes a network of learning centres; and the people themselves take control of their own and their family's whole-life learning. Museums, libraries, churches, businesses, YMCAs and a growing set of other learning centres, (mental fitness centres not unlike today's physical fitness centres), provide all citizens with the knowledge they need for their own right livelihood ... 'mentors' (whom we now call 'teachers') provide a personal consulting and advisory services to people of all ages. They keep detailed databases on learning opportunities throughout the region and by counselling and guidance help each family and individual reach self-set goals for gaining knowledge ..."

William. N. Ellis, Editor of TRANET

In *Smart Schools, Smart Kids,* (1992) Edward Fiske, New York Times educational editor, reports that US press correspondents met to review the results of five years of educational reform. They began to suspect that things were worse instead of better. Fiske went on tour to try to find something more positive. He concluded:

"Trying to get more learning out of the current system is like trying to get the Pony Express to compete with the telegraph by breeding faster ponies."

Fiske advocated a complete rethink of the fundamental assumptions of our obsolete model of schooling.

Sir Christopher Ball, Director of Learning for the Royal Society of Arts writing in the *RSA Journal,* December 1995, p.6, makes the following observation:

"I realised that I am among those who believe that Tomorrow's School will be a replacement for, not merely an adjustment of, today's system of education."

John Abbott, Director of Education 2000 in *Education 2000 News* September 1996, added his voice:

"Mounting evidence world-wide suggests that traditional education systems are becoming increasingly dysfunctional in the face of escalating technological, social, and economic change. Education systems based on out-of-date or incomplete assumptions about how people learn, can, unwittingly, create and perpetuate dependent societies. People who come to see themselves

as "learning failures" when young have no confidence in their ability to embrace change as adults."

Some industrial concerns in the USA are now supporting approaches with grants designed to:

"enable those entrepreneurs and risk-takers in education to break up the institutional gridlock that has stifled innovation and creativity."

These were the comments of Nabisco's chairman, Louis V. Gerstner.

In the Co-operative Society's Members magazine for Spring 1996, Byron Henderson, Director of the Centre for the Study of Co-operatives, Canada writes:

"Home schooling ... may well be at the forefront of school change ... The Wall Street Journal's electronic edition recently ran the story of a 13 year-old student in New York State who does not travel to a classroom, but instead uses his computer a third of his study day to access books, encyclopaedias on CD-ROM ... and the Internet, to meet friends, discuss classes and prepare reports ... Multi-media distance education and the Internet are coming to public awareness and they offer the prospect of both better education and lower cost."

John Taylor Gatto in his book *Dumbing Us Down: The Hidden Curriculum of Compulsory Schooling,* concludes that schooling in the USA is a twelve year jail sentence where, *"bad habits are the only curriculum truly learned",* and that school 'schools' very well, but hardly educates at all. It is time for drastic changes, he concludes.

As noted earlier, bullying is endemic in the model of schooling currently employed in UK because it operates as a **bully institution** - the compulsory day-prison, employs **a bully curriculum** - the compulsory National Curriculum, enforced by the increasingly favoured **bully pedagogy** of teacher-dominated formal teaching, and reinforced by the **bully compulsory assessment system**. In UK this is all reinforced by a **bully schools inspection service** led by a man who has declared in public meetings that *'fear is a great motivator'* - one of the classic doctrines of fascist-tending regimes that teaches that adults get their way by bullying - psychological, institutional, physical, or otherwise.

Alice Miller reminds us that every bully was once a victim, for bullying is learnt behaviour. Until we replace our current morbid model with a new model of a flexible learning system based on democratic principles, the root causes of bullying will continue.

1. Some key ideas for the next learning system

(a) Learner-managed learning

Home-schoolers rather take it for granted that the learners will manage their own learning, at first in style and soon after that in content. This is often achieved on a trial and error basis.

(b) A network of learning sites

In the proposed Minnesota Experimental City, planned as a laboratory for social, technical, economic and environmental innovations, a new approach to education is proposed. The following *Learning Centres* are to be developed to replace the current model of custodial schools:

- **Early life studios** will be designed so that parents, young children and staff members could meet regularly to create an environment that provided creative learning experiences and offer opportunities for parents and older young people and other adults to learn about the mental, emotional, physical and other needs of early childhood.

- **Stimulus studios** will be established where there would be a constantly changing array of prompts to provoke and extend learners' perceptions and thinking, to arouse curiosity, stimulate laughter, wonder, reverence, imagination and competence. There would be films, tapes, videos, exhibitions, books, resourceful people from the community, and virtual reality experiences.

- **Gaming studios** where learning takes place by playing educational games and there is the opportunity to take part in simulations and role play. Arena theatre events will also be developed and presented.

- **Project studios** will be available where learners work on real projects such as making a video, writing a book or TV script, designing new materials and products, or planning projects to be undertaken later in the community. In the UK, the Walsall Community Arts has produced a *Dreaming for Real* project pack which has been setting such projects in motion.

- **Learner banks** will be designed to store and loan out the tools and equipment needed by learners. A large part of the bank would store books and other material now found in conventional libraries.

- **Family-life centres** where families will learn together. The centre will offer meetings, seminars, tutoring or community centred discussions. Provision will be made here for those who learn well for some of the time in school-type settings.

- **Community facilities** such as homes, businesses, public places, sports facilities, would be available as appropriate, as part of the learning network. The network of learning centres will remain permanently fluid, open to evaluation, review and change. (see Glines, D. and Long K. (1992) "Transitioning Towards Educational Futures" *Phi Delta Kappen* March 1992).

In the new learning system, it is *learning* that is the central concern and not teaching. Every person is simultaneously a learner *and* a resource person for the learning of others.

When I was collecting information from home-schooling families in the late 1970s and 1980s, I found that I had to do most of my visits on Sundays. This was because whenever I telephoned to fix appointments, I would find that the learners were learning out-and-about in various libraries, museums, exhibitions, gatherings such as auctions, expeditions, sports centres, meetings with adults who had offered some learning opportunity, and the like. They had already taken on the idea of the community as a source of learning sites.

(c) The Catalogue Curriculum

When I wrote about the Catalogue Curriculum idea in 1995, Don Glines of the Educational Futures Project, USA, wrote about his experience of using such an approach in his US High School:

*"We found the 'window shopping and shopper's guide' notions helpful in the first year and for new students, but once the programme was rolling, the students just developed all their own studies and planned their own self-directed curriculum experiences ... even the 'low achievers' really take off when they finally learn that you **are** telling the truth - that they **can** create their own learning based upon interests and success."*

I can accept what Glines is saying here. When I gave student teachers choice about how to organise their initial teacher education course, the same thing happened - fifteen times in fifteen years. But 'the catalogue' enabled them to locate the best option for their purposes.

(d) Personal learning plans

The Royal Society of Arts has been promoting the idea of personal learning plans as part of its current educational initiative. The director, Sir Christopher Ball, sees the aim of the project as creating a learning culture in Britain. By implication, years of compulsory mass schooling have done no such thing, so something has to be done to reverse the trend.

(e) Direct access to the information-rich society

Seymour Papert in *Mindstorms* forecast how computer technology would change things by modifying the environment outside classrooms:

"I believe that the computer presence will enable us to so modify the learning environment outside the classroom that much, if not all, the knowledge schools presently try to teach with such pain and expense and such limited success will be learned, as the child learns to walk, painlessly, successfully, and without organised instruction.

This obviously implies that schools, as we know them today, will have no place in the future. But it is an open question whether they will adapt by transforming themselves into something new or wither away and be replaced."

(f) Teachers as learning agents

In John Adcock's book *In Place of Schools* he develops the idea of a new role for teachers. The model would be that of family doctors operating in health centres. The new teacher would not work in a school but in a centre, or from their homes, or both, and their concern would be to help devise and service the personal learning plans of a group of clients.

For my own part, I prefer a slightly different model - that of the travel agent. Teachers as learning agents would operate from their 'learning travel bureau' helping any learner to 'visit' and explore any learning that was chosen.

(g) Assessment on request

Philip Gammage observed that: *"Nobody grew taller by being measured."* This would seem to put assessment firmly in its place as a mass schooling fetish.

There are, however, several provisos. Systems such as the education systems of the Scandinavian countries certainly manage perfectly well without anything like external examinations such as the UK's GCSE and GCE 'A' levels. But they introduce vocational tests post-schooling on the sensible grounds that people who provide services in society need to be appropriately qualified; e.g. nobody I know wants their teeth attended to by unqualified people.

In addition, testing can be available on request. The grades for musical instrument proficiency are example of such tests. The 'on request' is, however, crucial. As a non music reading jazz musician myself, of somewhat modest achievement, the tests are no use to me, nor do I desire them. A compulsory testing system would, erroneously, identify me as a non-musician.

2. The old system and new system compared

With some key concepts now established, we can juxtapose the assumptions of the current compulsory mass schooling system with those of the next learning system.

The mass schooling system assumes that:

- Learning is preparation for life, so at some point learning stops and living starts.
- Learning occurs mostly in school.
- Specialists are needed to impart knowledge.
- Education takes place in a school and requires a prescribed curriculum.
- People do not and cannot learn on their own.
- People with a large quantity of memorised information are better people than those with less.
- Schools are needed to socialise and civilise.

The next learning system, on the other hand, assumes that:

- Learning is life, because humans are learning animals, and whilst we are alive, we are learning.
- Learning occurs everywhere and anywhere.
- People can direct their own learning.
- Education is a lifelong activity that needs to be personalised using a catalogue curriculum.
- People can learn to make decisions on what and how to learn.
- Everyone is important regardless of how much they have memorised.
- People are socialised and get civilised in their communities.

The trailblazing activity of the home-schoolers now begins to become clear because they have already been 'field testing' most of the components of the new system for almost twenty years, without necessarily having this as a conscious intention.

3. Home-schoolers in co-operation

Some home-schooling families are already busily developing learning clubs, family centres and other forms of co-operative learning as the following accounts demonstrate:

(a) The Otherwise Club

"In February 1993 we set up The Otherwise Club as a centre for families of children educated out of school and committed to some vision of alternative education. It evolved out of a small learning club at one parent's house in which children from home-based educating families were able to work together regularly on interesting projects. The group was set up with two basic aims:

- to provide for regular social interaction where families can exchange views and ideas. This is something we feel causes concern to those considering home education.

- to provide workshops and group activities in which members can participate. This aspect of educating out of school for many families requires most effort and organisation.

Our premises are at the Carlton Centre, Kilburn where we hire a hall and several rooms and a kitchen for two days a week. There are also specialist areas for woodwork, photographic developing and pottery available. We have about 20 families who pay £100 per year to cover basic costs. Workshops have been enjoyed on first aid, philosophy for children and stained glass work. Forthcoming workshops include computers and rock climbing. Drama, pottery and the production of a newsletter are regular activities. Parents talking to parents and exchanging experiences about home-based education is a regular but non-scheduled vital activity. The whole family can learn together and also socialise with other families.

The Otherwise Club is run collectively, with all members having equal access to setting the agenda and to the decision-making process. There is a fortnightly meeting and a key planning meeting every half term."

(Above extract is from the leaflet describing The Otherwise Club which can be obtained by sending a stamped addressed envelope (20p) to: Leslie Barson. 1 Croxley Road, London W1 3HH)

(b) The Brambles Centre

"At Brambles and our MAGIC Resource Centre, we are actively involved in de-schooling. All the families in the Co-op are home-educating. We see learning as a lifelong adventure that involves young people and adults equally. As well as living in the Co-op with our young people who do not attend school, we also offer support and advice to others who are de-schooling or thinking about it.

Education is a term that is very open to individual interpretations; but as the law currently stands every child has the right to an education. Whether this happens in a school or 'otherwise', e.g. through home-based learning, is, however, a matter of choice. We choose the home-based education alternative.

We want to see people taking control of their lives and working together to build a more sustainable world. Children who learn naturally in a supportive community, rather than being artificially taught by someone imposed on them, generally grow in confidence, become more self-sufficient and want to learn new skills.

Brambles was set up by a small group of unemployed people. Based in Sheffield, it is a registered non-profit-making housing co-operative that enables us to house ourselves and others on low incomes. More and more people are realising that we can take control of our lives without bosses and landlords and create a sustainable future through co-operation and mutual aid. On the ground floor of one of the houses is a resource centre for use by the co-operative and a base for our home-based education and it is also used by other groups in the community."

Extract from a leaflet which can be obtained from:
Brambles Housing Co-operative, 82 Andover Street, Sheffield, S3 9EH, enclosing a stamped addressed C5 envelope.

(c) Flexi-time schooling

Flexi-time is part-time attendance at school using schools just as they are. It can be seen as a temporary expedient for those who cannot wait for a new system to get established, but for various reasons, do not want to home-educate full-time.

School becomes one of many resources, such as libraries, radio, television, computers, etc., to be used when the child and parent choose, according to a contract between them and the school. The parents are as equally involved as the teachers in the education of the child, whilst the children are encouraged to learn for themselves as well as being taught.

Any school can accommodate flexi-time if its wishes to, but under current law, no school is obliged to. ... The Education Act 1993 (Part IV, subsection 298, No.4) applies:

"A local education authority may make arrangements for the provision of suitable full-time or part-time education otherwise than at school for those young persons who, by reason of illness, exclusion from school or otherwise, may not for any period receive suitable education unless such arrangements are made for them."

Kate Oliver writes of her experience:

"At the school where my children attend on an agreed flexi-time basis, they are recorded as 'educated off-site' which is classified as an 'authorised absence'. This means that the funding is exactly as for a full-time student and the school returns are not affected. In the USA, however, the funding is split between the school and the home in the 'Independent Study Programs', as such arrangements are called. In California, specially trained staff work out appropriate flexible study plans with the parents and children who want this arrangement. Thus a personal learning plan or learning contract formalises the practical arrangements as regards attendance and learning activity. I also agreed to serve as a school governor."

(Kate Oliver is willing to share her experiences of negotiating and implementing flexi-time schooling. Write to her at 21 St. Mary's Crescent, Leamington Spa, CV31 1JL)

(d) The Open School project

Open School is a non-profit making charity started by Lord Young of Dartington in 1989 to make the methods of the Open University available to young students, especially those not in attendance at school for whatever reason. Its major initiative is tele-tutoring by fax as a new development in distance learning. It provides services for hospital education, traveller groups and families educating at home.

Courses are provided for both examination and non-examination work. GCSE courses are available including Maths, English, Sociology, Psychology, Law, Accounting, Spanish, French and German. GCE A-level courses are available in English, Maths, Sociology and Psychology.

(Information can be obtained from Open School, Park Road, Dartington Hall, Devon, TG9 6EQ Tel: 01803 866542 Fax: 01803 866676)

(e) Uppattinas Educational Resource Centre

The re-creation of the Uppattinas school came after a long and painful struggle when the members faced up to the fact that there just were not enough students who could pay sufficient tuition fees, or families who could work hard enough to make up for the shortfall in finances, to sustain the needs of the physical plant, or the teachers required for maintaining it as a 'school'. But it was possible to sustain the physical plant and preserve the integrity of its original commitment to open education through establishing it as a Learning Resource Centre which could be a 'school' or 'un-school', depending on the needs of the members. The director of the centre, Sandy Hurst, explained:

> *"That was a direction in which I was headed personally
> and something into which I could put the energy needed
> for organisation and direction. This could once again be
> a place to which people came who truly wanted to learn
> and to share what they had learned."*

Based on the idea that we learn everywhere so school is everywhere, then the new Uppattinas is a part of that learning and is still a school. It continues to be a centre for people who want to make contact with others, for learning and sharing, for doing group projects or individual projects, for meeting and for growing together. It is not circumscribed by age limits or time limits. Everyone is welcome and the facility is open to community members as and when they need it. Programmes are limited only by the interests and needs of those involved.

The centre of activities has become families who educate their children at home and use the centre to augment their programmes of study, and students who come to the centre for classes.

Workshops and special activities like music and drama are arranged as they are needed by the community. Facilities are available for group meetings large and small, and for many kinds of activities for people of all ages. Workshops have been organised ranging from music improvisation to American Indian survival skills; projects on a variety of environmental concerns; and classes spanning American Literature to First Aid. A list of teachers available to those who need them is kept up-to-date.

The work of the centre is growing and developing and its members currently see it as,

> *"a doing centre for all ages, a repository for tools for doing things, a repository for records of things done, a place for sharing, a source of helpers, a centre for people from all cultures, a source for participant controlled learning, a centre for all who believe in life-long learning."*

(Uppattinas Educational Resource Centre, Glenmoore, PA, USA as described in *The Freethinkers' Pocket Directory to the Educational Universe*, Educational Heretics Press 1995)

(f) Oaklands Educational Resource Centre

Oaklands is a former Sunday School which then grew into a village school, and has now been recycled and re-opened as both the family home of Anne and Kathy Mills and Michael Robinson, and as a resource centre for home-educating families. As the Oaklands newsletter of December 1996 explains:

> *"Home-educating families are taking a significant step towards creating an optimistic vision of the future of education, by enacting a highly flexible education system which is able to meet the individual needs of each unique family and child. 'Education Otherwise' forms a valuable network helping us link together to support each other - Oaklands Educational Resource Centre can offer whatever else we choose to create, to make home-education the very best for ourselves and our children. Oaklands will also extend its educaional facilities beyond the home-education network, to provide a variety of courses and workshops for adults, plus activities for*

> *children and adults to enjoy together, as well as*
> *providing a venue to hire, for other people or*
> *organisations whose aims or values are aligned with our*
> *own."*

(Oaklands is in the village of Airmyn in East Yorkshire, UK and further details may be obtained from Anne Mills, Oaklands, High Street, Airmyn, Near Goole, East Yorkshire, DN14 8BF)

Summary

Some of the components of the next learning system are now becoming clearer, and they include:

* Learner-managed learning;

* A network of learning sites;

* The catalogue curriculum;

* Personal learning plans;

* Direct access to the information-rich society;

* Teachers as learning agents;

* Parents as 'residential' learning agents;

* Assessment on request.

The change in approach has begun to be noted:

> *"In the 20th century, provision has come before clients.*
> *You designed the courses and then tried to find some*
> *students to fill them. It is the other way round in the*
> *future: find the clients, find out what they want and need*
> *and then design (or redesign) your provision."*

(Sir Christopher Ball, in RSA Journal, Nov. 1966, p.9)

As the evidence in this book suggests, the home-schoolers are well ahead in developing and field-testing many of the features listed above. Indeed, they are blazing a trail to the next learning system and it is high time we learnt some important lessons from their success.

References and Reading

Abbott, J. (1996) 'The search for next-century learning' *Education 2000 News*

Adcock, J. (1994) *In Place of Schools* London: New Education

Alaska Department of Education (1985) *SRA Survey of Basic Skills, Alaska Statewide Assessment* Spring 1985 Juneau A.K.: Author, and (1986) *Results from 1981 CAT (For CCS)* Juneau A.K.: Author

Chapman, J., Froumin, I., and Aspin, D. (1995) *Creating and Managing the Democratic School* London: Falmer

Davies, L. (1994) *Beyond Authoritarian School Management* Ticknall: Education Now Books

Fiske, E. B. (1992) *Smart Schools, Smart Kids* New York; Touchstone

Gardner, H. (1991) *The Unschooled Mind* London: Fontana

Gatto, J. T. (1992) *Dumbing Us Down: The Hidden Curriculum of Compulsory Schooling* Philadelphia: New Society

Glines, D. (1995) *Creating Educational Futures* Michigan: McNaughton and Gunn

Handy, C. (1990) *The Age of Unreason* London: Arrow

Havens, J. E. (1994) 'Parent educational levels as they relate to academic achievement among home schooled children.' *Home School Researcher* Vol.10, No. 4.

Hewitt Research Foundation (1985) 'North Dakota trial results pending' *Parent Educator and Family Report* 3, 2 p.5.

Hewitt Research Foundation (1986) 'Study of homeschoolers taken to court '*Parent Educator and Family Report* 4, 1, p.2.

Holmes, E. (1911) *What Is and What Might Have Been* London: Constable

Holt, J. (1971) *The Underachieving School* Harmondsworth: Penguin

Holt, J. (1972) *Freedom and Beyond* New York: E.P.Dutton & Co

Holt, J. (1975) *Escape From Childhood* Harmondsworth: Penguin

Holt, J. (1982) *Teach Your Own* Brightlingsea: Lighthouse Books

Holt, J. (1991) *Learning All the Time* Ticknall: Education Now

Hornick, J. (1993) 'Science instruction of home schooled teenagers' *Home School Researcher* Vol. 9, No. 1.

Knowles, J. G. (1993) 'Homeschooling and socialisation' Michigan: University of Michigan School of Education Study Press Release

Lowden, S. (1993) *The Scope and Implications of Home-based Education* Ph.D Thesis, University of Nottingham

Marchant, G. (1993) Home schoolers on-line *Home School Researcher* Vol 9, No. 2.

Mayberry, M., Knowles, J.G., Ray, B., and Marlow, S. (1995) *Home Schooling: Parents as Educators* Thousand Oaks, California: Corwin Press

Meighan, R. (1984) 'Home-based educators and Education Authorities : the attempt to maintain a mythology' *Educational Studies* Vol. 10, No. 3.

Meighan, R. (1988) *Flexischooling,* Ticknall: Education Now Books

Meighan, R. ed., (1992) *Learning from Home-based Education,* Ticknall: Education Now Books

Meighan, R. (1993) *Theory and Practice of Regressive Education,* Nottingham: Educational Heretics Press

Meighan, R., with J. Meighan (ed) (1995) *The Freethinkers' Pocket Directory to the Educational Universe* Nottingham: Educational Heretics Press

North, R. (1987) *Schools of Tomorrow* Hartland: Green Books

Papert, S. (1980) *Mindstorms: Children, Computers and Powerful Ideas* London: Harvester Press

Ray, B. D. (1991) *A Nationwide Study of Home Education: Family Characteristics, Legal Matters and Student Achievement* Seattle, WA: National Education Research Institute

Rogers, C. (1983) *Freedom to Learn in the 80s* Columbus, Ohio: Merrill

Rose, C., and Nicholl, M.J. (1997) *Accelerated Learning for the 21st Century* (forthcoming)

Russell, T.J. (1994) 'Cross-validation of a Multi-variate Path Analysis of Predictors of Home School Student Academic Achievement' *Home School Researcher* Vol.10, No.1.

Sande, J. (1995) 'The Impact of Homeschooling on Math Education' *Home School Researcher* Vol. 11, No. 3.

Sherman, A. (1996) *Rules, Routines and Regimentation* Nottingham: Educational Heretics Press

Shute, C. (1993) *Compulsory Schooling Disease* Nottingham: Educational Heretics Press

Shute, C. (1994) *Alice Miller: The Unkind Society, Parenting and Schooling* Nottingham: Educational Heretics Press

Shyers, L. (1992) 'A comparison of social adjustment between home and traditionally schooled students' *Home School Researcher* Vol. 8, No. 3.

Smedley, T. (1992) 'Socialisation of home school children' *Home School Researcher* Vol. 8, No. 3.

Smith, D. S. (1993) *Parent-generated Home Study in Canada* New Brunswick: The Francombe Place

Thomas, A. (1994) 'The quality of learning experienced by children who are educated at home.' paper given at *British Psychological Society Annual Conference*

Tillman, V.D. (1995) 'Home Schoolers, Self Esteem,and Socialisation' *Home School Researcher* Vol. 11, No.3.

Webb, J. (1990) *Children Learning at Home* Brighton: Falmer Press

Wells, G. (1986) *The Meaning Makers: Children Learning Language and Using Language to Learn* London: Hodder and Stoughton

Appendix One:

When schools are gone ...

In another vision of educational futures, John Adcock tells the story of how a new system came into being in the UK in his book *In Place of Schools:*

"It is Friday, 28th December in the year 2029. The hour is 0808 EST (European Standard Time) Susan Smith checks this on her personal computer screen together with the local weather and traffic news, and her day's appointments. Susan, born in the first hour of the first year of the 21st century, is a professional personal tutor to nineteen children aged from eight to ten years.

She tutors the children with their parents, or in small groups, in their homes, in her home, in community resource centres, in field stations, in museums and art galleries, in concert halls and theatres, in libraries and sports centres, and in other places where, in her professional opinion, advantage to her clients will accrue.

Susan is not a teacher in the 19th or 20th century sense of the word. She does not teach in a school. There are no teachers and there are no schools. There are simply personal tutors, pupils, parents and extensive support facilities.

Susan possesses for each of the children in her tutorial group a personal study programme. She devised each programme with the help of the child, his parents, and colleagues notes on the child's earlier achievements."

John Adcock (1996) **In Place of Schools,** New Education Press,

ISBN 0-946947-62-7 price £5-95

Appendix Two:
The Flexi College Initiative

The education system of the 21st century is likely to see a radical replacement of the existing authoritarian school by a new kind of learning system. This will feature flexi-time use of some existing school buildings, and new resource centres for use by home-based educating families, to create a regenerated education system in which person-centred learning in democratic and co-operative groupings enables a wider diversity of provision, to meet the needs of individuals for creative self-development within the new moral constraints of the current human predicament. Flexi College is designed to be an adaptable model of such a school.

The East Midlands Flexi College has grown out of Philip Toogood's previous 20 years of work in mini-schooled large comprehensives, small schools and community education. A carefully researched proposal was produced in 1991 with Richard Terry, now one of the 4 tutors in the group flexi-teaching partnership working at the flexible learning centre at Monk Street, Tutbury, North Staffordshire. Here parents, teachers, students and local people contract together in an education venture at the heart of which is a small flexible school for students from 8 to 16 years old. For the future, a 16 to 19 years group is planned and the Flexi College will be complete when an early childhood section is added later. This cluster of small groups, served by a flexi-teaching partnership, will be run by a limited company with charitable status.

In 1996, the East Midlands Flexi College took the bold step of setting up a training company, Stakeholder Training Initiatives Ltd, in information technology whose profits would largely be devoted towards keeping the Flexi College low cost and independent. Stakeholder was conceived as a full business to be commercially run nation-wide. Once Stakeholder Training Initiatives was in place, a partnership was established with Bilston Community College, under the forward-thinking directorship of Keith Wymer, towards implementing the joint aims of Bilston and Flexi College. Thus, Flexi College was poised at the outset of 1997, to take off as an important contribution to local systems of education, especially relevant to inner cities and areas of high deprivation. This is not to assert, however, that Flexi College is an 'alternative' in the sense of remedial provision. **All** students would benefit from this shift of emphasis away from the authoritarian imprisoning school to the empowerment of the membership of a small co-operative learning group. Flexi College contains the seed of a radical idea which could rapidly transform the whole system of education.

Meanwhile at East Midlands Flexi College, 17 students and teachers start each day with exercises, a review of world affairs, meetings to plan the day, mornings of intensive small group directed work in Maths, English, Science, Information Technology, and French, afternoons of long autonomous tutor-supported sessions in Art, Design, Expressive Arts, and Humanities and finish each day with supported Independent Study sessions. Local facilities of libraries, sports centres and the local countryside are used as resources. GCSE, 'A' level, GNVQ and NVQ examinations are on offer. The year is framed into 6 modules containing 6 symposium presentation weeks, 3 Expressive Arts evenings, 3 expeditions and 3 specially negotiated activity weeks. Parents, students, tutors and local people can join a Life-long Learning Association. A Wider Horizons Club operates out of school hours and will be extended into all kinds of after-school, weekend, and holiday courses. By co-operative work, funds are raised and practical maintenance done.

A Flexi College is fundamentally a network of centres where people can join small learning groups, or work independently, and can gain access to the support, advice and tuition of professional tutors. These tutors work in group practices which respond to the needs of people for lifelong learning, a widening of their horizons and for flexible learning groups with which to share their learning experiences. These centres may be of three sorts. They may be free-standing, or part of a cluster, or a federation of small learning groups (or 'mini-schools') on one campus site. In our information rich society it is a system built on such active participation in democratic learning which holds out the best hope of the widest number of people being able to take part in the joy and fulfilment of learning, a consummation which most systems hitherto have only been able to offer to only a small privileged minority.

(For further information, send stamped addressed envelope to: Philip Toogood, East Midlands Flexi College Ltd , Monk Street, Tutbury, Staffs, DE13 9NA or telephone/fax 01283 520714)

Appendix Three:

Home-based Education - Basic Questions

Is it legal?

Yes - it is the *parent's* duty to ensure that the child receives a proper education. To do this, they may choose to use schools or to educate at home. Children of all ages can and do learn at home.

Do I have to inform the Local Education Authority?

No - if your child has never been registered at a state school.
Yes - by writing to inform the head teacher, if you are withdrawing your child from a state school. This is your *right* - you do not need 'approval' to do it.

Do I have to follow the National Curriculum?

No - the law states that children may be educated according to the wishes of the parent(s). Independent schools are also exempt, and so are parents in Scotland.

Will my child have to take the SATs?

No - formal testing is not required. The Local Education Authority may ask to send an inspector to monitor progress. You do not have to agree, but a family in a court judgement was said to be behaving unreasonably, but not unlawfully, when it did not. (Harrison v. Stevenson 1981)

Can GCSEs and 'A'-levels be taken at home?

Yes - many young people enter as external candidates, or arrange for part-time attendance at Further Education College. Some have taken 'A'-levels when they were ready, the youngest being 10 years of age, and not bothered with the GCSE stage at all.

Is home-based education costly?

No - some single parents educate their children at home on income support. You do not need expensive equipment. Radio, TV, broadsheet newspapers, free information booklets, and books from the local library are all part of our information-rich society and rich sources of learning.

Are the children deprived of a social life?

No - the home is useful as a springboard for learning excursions out and about in the community when the children mix with all ages. Home-based educating families also meet regularly for joint activities. The research shows that it is children at school who are less socially skilled, less mature and less personally confident. They are, after all, confined for 15,000 hours with the limited resources of their peer group.

Do I have to be a teacher?

No - Many parents learn alongside their children so the whole family benefits from the experience. Encouragement, enthusiasm, and support for a 'finding out' approach are all useful attributes.

Can you study science at home?

Yes - Open University students do it in their thousands. The equipment needed can often be improvised or sometimes shared with other families or borrowed.

Can a child with a Statement for Special Educational Needs be educated at home?

Yes - The Local Education Authority must make provision unless the parent or parents have made "suitable arrangements" at home (Education Act 1981, section 2). One LEA has given a grant of £2000 per child per annum to a particular family for this to happen at home.

Can the Local Education Authority tell me **how** to home-educate?

No - you have a choice of approaches and a bitter court case was fought over this precise issue. Judgement was given against an LEA trying to impose its school-type vision on a family (see Harrison v. Stevenson 1981).

Contacts: (please send C5 size S.A.E. in all cases)
Education Otherwise, P.O. Box 7420, London N9 9SG
Home Education Advisory Service,
5 Elm Gardens, Welwyn Garden City, Herts AL8 6RX
Education Now,
113 Arundel Drive, Bramcote Hills, Nottingham NG9 3FQ